Job Interview Skills

By Doris Ehigie

Published by New Generation Publishing in 2014

Copyright © Doris Ehigie 2014

First Edition

The author asserts the moral right under the Copyright, Designs and Patents Act 1988 to be identified as the author of this work.

All Rights reserved. No part of this publication may be reproduced, stored in a retrieval system or transmitted, in any form or by any means without the prior consent of the author, nor be otherwise circulated in any form of binding or cover other than that which it is published and without a similar condition being imposed on the subsequent purchaser.

www.newgeneration-publishing.com

 **New Generation Publishing**

Acknowledgements

Special thanks to my husband for assisting in editing this book and my children for their understanding and patience.

Contents

Acknowledgements	3
Contents	4
Introduction	5
What is a job interview?	6
Types of Interviews	6
Interview Effectiveness	8
Before the interview	10
At the interview	12
Dos and Don'ts at an Interview	14
Recognizing your skills and qualities	15
Differentiate skills from qualities	15
Interview Questions and Answering Hints	17
After the interview	21
Essential requirements for application form	22
CV Composure	23
Conclusion	24
Bibliography	25

Introduction

At some point in life, people will need to attend a job interview. Hence, this book is written and targeted to anyone looking to acquire essential skills to work. Also it covers valuable information such as what you will require to have on your application form and CV (Curriculum Vitae).

You may have attended an interview before but seeking to brush your interview skills or you have just graduated and about searching for jobs to apply for or you may have been unemployed for a long time and looking to get your way back to employment, the information entailed in this book will help you understand relevant steps needed to prepare you to stand best chance of success during an interview.

First of all, it is imperative to start by defining the meaning of a job interview.

What is a job interview?

A job interview is a dialogue between a representative of a company and a candidate who has applied for that job.

Types of Interviews

There are different types of interviews, which are: Group interviews, Telephone interviews, Panel interviews, One to one interview, Competency based interviews, etc.

Group interview:
This is when you are invited to be assessed as part of a group; sometimes an interviewer may use this to test how you might work as part of a team. Therefore it is important for you to know what team work is and be ready to play an active role by participating in-group discussion.

Telephone interview: An employer may use a telephone interview to assess your communication skills also how you might deal with someone on the phone, so be prepared and have your CV or application form handy at that given point so that you have something to re-cap from.

One to One Interview: This is when one person is interviewing a candidate only. Sometimes some private organizations may use this method.

Panel Interview: This method of interviewing is normally common, most especially in the public sector, it involves two or more interviewers interviewing an applicant, this approach is very good and can eliminate bias.

Competency based interviews: This type of interview is when you are required to describe your skills and experience in detailed using some good examples to support your answers. For example you may want to talk about your ICT skills describing how you have used a certain Microsoft package such as Word, Excel, PowerPoint or Database application to achieve a certain task.

Make sure you know the type of interview you are called for and prepare well in advance.

Haven carefully outlined the different types of interviews mentioned above; the next phase will be to discuss interview effectiveness and what you need to be aware of to enable you plan very well.

Interview Effectiveness

For you to be successful in an interview you need to ensure proper preparation and planning in order to prevent a poor performance. Have a look at the triangle below

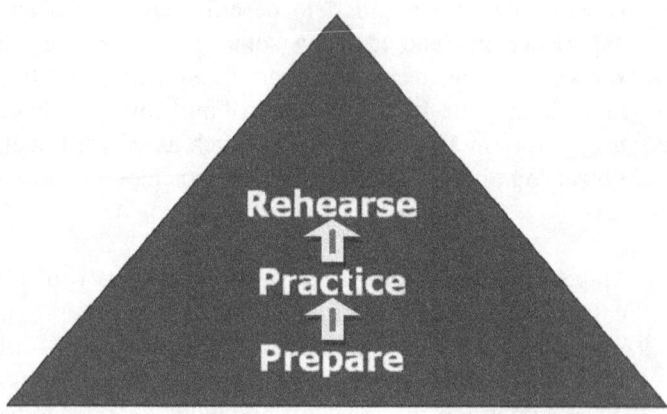

The diagram projected above reflects on three things which means you have to

Prepare, practice and rehearse: you will need to prepare as well as practice for questions that may likely come out during an interview. If possible get someone to do a mock interview for you while others observe the way you respond to questions, quality of answers given, the tone of voice used, body language displayed during the interview etc. Practice and rehearsing as many times as possible can make you feel better and more confident.

An interview can be successful when you plan your schedule effectively.

The next step is to ascertain what you need to prepare for before you attend an interview.

Before the interview

Note that when you are invited to attend an interview, it means you are one step closer to getting that job but you still need to plan the following carefully:

- ❖ Prepare yourself by making sure you have read your application form or CV over and over again. Understand your strengths and weaknesses but emphasis on your strength more.

- ❖ Do a research about the organisation by requesting information pack in advance or visit the company website if they have one to obtain more information, know what they do, the services they provide etc.

- ❖ Put together information you will need to take along with you on the day e.g. your credentials such as certificates, ID, etc if requested by the employer or not.

- ❖ Read through the Job description - the duties about the job role also the person specification that is the knowledge and experience required.

- ❖ Plan your journey well in advanced, do not assume it, if possible do a dummy run of the location before you attend your interview so as to avoid any delay on that particular day, also have a plan B in case you are delayed by transportation or any other emergency occurrence; ensure you have the employer phone number to call.

❖ A tidy appearance is vital, don't overlook it, dress smart and make sure your clothes are neat.

The following chapter will explain what you should be aware of at the interview

At the interview

- ❖ Timing is very crucial so ensure you are prompt, aim to arrive at least 10 minutes to 15 minutes before your interview commence.

- ❖ Handshake: Sometimes an interviewer may offer his or her hand, so feel free to shake them with confidence.

- ❖ First Impression really counts: Make sure you present yourself appropriately. Though one can be nervous sometimes but relax as much as possible and be at ease at all times. Also practice some good breathing techniques to help you calm down.

Be aware of your Body Language as this plays an important function during an interview. For example:

- ➢ **Posture**: Ensure you have a balanced posture by sitting up straight and well back in your chair with your hands and body relaxed, avoid fiddling or touching things.

- ➢ **Eye contact**: Look at the interviewer in the eye but do not stair at them because a good eye contact shows that you are listening and interested in the job, also it shows that you have a good rapport with the interviewer.

➢ **Facial expression:** Smile when necessary, do not show unhappiness even if you do not understand anything because when you smile it shows that you are confident and relaxed.

➢ **Voice**: Make sure you speak in a clear voice everyone can understand.

The next chapter will explain interview *dos* and *don'ts*.

Dos and Don'ts at an Interview

The following table below outline what you should do and not do during an interview

Dos	Don'ts
Be composed and confident	Don't show nervousness or draw attention to your weaknesses
Try and speak clearly, be positive and enthusiastic	Avoid the use of jargon, such as you knows
Listen carefully to questions and ask for clarity if unsure	Don't wobble or swear or criticise anyone
Sell yourself and take time to answer questions with some examples	Don't rush answers and don't chew gum during the interview
Be honest	Don't lie about your answers

Recognizing your skills and qualities

It is important for you to know your strengths by figuring out your skills and qualities. Skills are what you learnt and can do e.g. ICT skills while qualities are what you have inside of you for example you could be energetic, a careful person and so on.

Take a look at this short exercise on skills and qualities and see if you can

Differentiate skills from qualities

	Skills - Please √	Qualities - Please √
Communication		
Problem Solving		
Reliable		
Calm		
Singing		
Organization		
Drawing & Painting		
Patience		
Confident		
Hardworking		

Haven practiced and analysed your skills and qualities from the table above, it is vital to prepare further by practicing some common questions that might arise during an interview. An Interviewer may use questions to find out your understanding about the job also to gather information on how your previous experience relates to the position you have applied for.

Interview Questions and Answering Hints

An employer may ask you the following questions:

✓ Could you tell me a bit about yourself?

Hint in answering:
Talk about your career and some work experience you have done, it could be current or in the past.

✓ Why do you want to work in this organisation?

Hint in answering:
It is a good idea to research the company beforehand and try to relate what interest you to what the company does. You may want to say things like the company equal opportunity policy is fair to all, you will like to work for this organisation because their reputation is very good etc.

✓ Why have you applied for this post and what skills and qualities do you have to offer?

Hint in answering:
Demonstrate an interest in the job, talk about the skills & qualities you possess.

✓ Have you done this kind of work before?

Hint in answering:
If you have done the kind of work before provide examples of when you did, if you have not, you can describe your previous work experience and relate it to the job.

✓ Why should the employer take you on?
Hint in answering:
Tell them you are capable for this job; try demonstrating your strengths, that is, what you are good at and relate it to the position you have applied for.

✓ How do you know that you are delivering quality service?
Hint in answering:
Mention customer satisfaction, survey / feedback.

✓ Do you have any ICT experience?
Hint in answering:
Give examples of any Microsoft IT packages you can use with a brief description.

✓ What are your strengths and weaknesses?
Hint in answering:
Emphasis your strengths, qualities and give examples of what you can do but don't draw too much attention to your weaknesses.

✓ What is your understanding about teamwork?
Hint in answering:
Ensure you understand what team work is: Teamwork involves two or more people working together to achieve a common goal. Explain when you have worked as part of team and how you contributed to accomplish success.

Interviewers normally request if you have any questions you would like to ask?

So prepare questions to ask in advance, show interest in the job for example you may want to ask the interviewers the following:
- Are there opportunities for personal development?
- Would I be working in a team?
- Will there be a period of induction etc.?

Be aware that some interview process comes with some testing categories such as:

- Presentation – this is when you have to present a given task using a PowerPoint slides or a Flip chart.

- In-tray exercise – Sometimes you may be given a scenario or exercise to do, for example an exercise such as describing a situation when you had to organise or manage a project.

- IT test – you may be tested on ICT applications such as Word, Excel, and PowerPoint, Access etc.

- Basic skills testing – sometimes this may take the form of Numeracy and Literacy to test your knowledge.

- Personality test – This can be in form of how you may react in a given situation, for example how you might handle multiple workloads at the same time.

- Aptitude test: for instance how you may reason with numbers, follow instructions and solve problems etc.

Ensure you find out if your interview will involve any of the above tests and prepare properly.

After the interview

After the interview, it is a good idea to thank the panel and then make a Professional Exit. Also remember to take note of what went well and what didn't go well to help you identify any area you may improve on.

Having completed the process to ensure success at a job interview, we will now look at:

Essential requirements for application form

To complete an application form, you will need to address the following area carefully:

- Make sure you supply accurate personal details of yourself.

- State your relevant Qualifications and work Employment history.

- Address the Personal Statement by matching your work experience with some good examples.

- Provide good references.

- Ensure your application is clear, neat and pay attention to instructions such as using Black ink, writing in Block format etc.

- Check the deadline to submit your form and ensure it is sent off on time.

CV Composure

The word CV is an abbreviation; it is called **CURRICULUM VITAE**. It entails information about you and normally includes the following data:

Personal details e.g. Your Name, Address, Date of Birth.
Email, Telephone / mobile number
Education and Training
Work / Voluntary Experience
Hobbies / Interests
References - this can be available on request.

When composing a CV, make sure these areas mentioned above are covered. Make your CV interesting, always proof read your work by ensuring you check the spelling and grammar. Also don't use more than two sides of A4, one sheet is normally of good length but don't over crowd it.

Conclusion

Proper preparation is vital for success. This book has explained essential skills required, the how and more to prepare you for the world of work.
　Best wishes!

Bibliography

http://www.cipd.co.uk/hr-careers/explore-hr-careers/interview-tips.htm

https://nationalcareersservice.direct.gov.uk/advice/getajob/interviews/Pages/default.aspx

http://www.recruitmentstream.com/hr-blog/

www.ingramcontent.com/pod-product-compliance
Lightning Source LLC
LaVergne TN
LVHW041526070426
835507LV00013B/1852